The Map

By
Kathryn Clarke

The Map
By Kathryn Clarke

ISBN: 978-0-9835597-6-4

Publisher:
Gabriel Press
www.gabrielpressusa.com

Illustrations by Devlin Fay
www.devlinfay.com

Contents

Introduction

When people were lost, in the days before instant hand-held technology, they often stopped at gas stations and bought road maps. In our time, there are many who are spiritually lost. Despite travelling at break-neck speed through life, they never find spiritual safety and joy. People need God.

In this time, there may be more people away from a church than inside of a church. Some call these people fallen-aways. Some of the people themselves might say they are runaways. Regardless, they are spiritual beings without benefit of a faith community. Many are non-practicing Catholics.

This writing does not seek to proclaim judgment on anyone's life choices, or, more accurately at times, anyone's circumstances, predicaments, quagmires or quandaries. (Nobody likes that guy.) But we do need to get to God inside us. And so, I offer a map of sorts.

Now, with regard to maps, they can be funny things. And we all know that some people will follow the map strictly and some only look at the map so they can decide which way they will *not* go. They like to do things their own way. And some maps are not up to date. But **this map** is state of the art. It will not become obsolete because it is going to do something very current. It is going to immediately reconfigure with the reader at each moment of his journey, and direct him back to the best road. The only maps known to do that are the maps connected to satellites, which are sources of information which seem far away but which are actually reassuringly close. They grab our location within seconds of our every wrong turn. This map reconfigures at every wrong turn also, only the satellite is God.

Let's stay with the introduction first. Some people will skip these next paragraphs because they skip all introductions. They don't have time for introductions or instructions. And then later, they go back and see what created a sag in their effort. But this paragraph and the ones which come next are important. (If you really do not have time, just read the last sentences.) This is why. This paragraph includes a simple statement of fact: You need this map.

Some people will huff and puff at that statement. "How dare anyone tell me what I need," they object. "I need nothing. I have my skills, some money. I have my family, my intelligence and love and that is all I need." Now it is good when things are going well for people and they have all of those things. But the experience of security can vanish like smoke after a fireworks display. Even faster. Because the truth is that all of those things are gifts from God and we can lose those things at any moment. Why? Because God is mean? Spiteful? No. It is because these gifts are temporary. Any gifts we are given, we are given for a purpose, divine in nature. And here is another irrefutable truth. Whether we dwell on it or not, we are on a journey that will end in death. The point of this second paragraph? Your destination in life, like it or not, is death.

"This writer is depressing," you may protest. "She can keep her map." But my friends, please, before you put down this map, reread the last two sentences of the last two paragraphs and then make an act of belief that this writer is not telling lies. You need this map. Not just because death awaits you. Let me reframe it. More cheerfully, life eternal awaits you.

Please understand, this map will not lecture, berate, condemn, judge, act in a superior fashion, list rules, look down on you, examine you for flaws, talk about you behind your back or tell you to hurry up. This map is patient and kind, understanding and peaceful. This map has a great feature though, one that becomes more effective the longer you follow it. The map acts like a mirror. It reflects the true you back to you. So while others are talking, talking, and talking. And still others are searching, searching and searching. You can be looking at this map and travelling as quickly or as slowly as you like and gradually, over time, maybe hours, maybe weeks, maybe years, learning all about the beauty of <u>you</u>. Then, you will discover that you only barely understand the vast amount of goodness you have access to in your heart.

Yes, you are fabulous. And this map, if followed, will show you how to smile with a smile that comes from deep within you and reaches all the way to your eyes. And when others see you smiling at them this way, they will smile, too, because you will be showing them that they, too, are fabulous and delightful. And people will know that whoever they are, whatever they are doing, they fit in with you. Why? People will feel happy around you because you are following the map.

Now, be warned. There is nobody else on your road. Therefore, any racing or competitive behavior will make you look ridiculous. If someone jumps out at you and begins competing with you, well, they are just embarrassing themselves. Look away politely. With regard to competition and racing ... it's just not that kind of map.

To conclude the introduction, the map is washable. It does not hold dirt and a simple wipe will restore it. It is not the kind of map that folds either because who could handle that job? How many people trying to refold a map were tempted to scrunch it up in a ball and shove it in the glove compartment, and then, using their foot, slam that closed? It was other maps which prompted an oppositional defiant disorder. Do not be tempted against this map. It is self-folding and meant to be used by less than perfectly clean hands. But let me make one more point. If you use this map at all, you will advance.

To summarize the introduction, we take the last sentences of the paragraphs above.

People need God. And so I offer a map of sorts. This map reconfigures at every wrong turn only the satellite is God. You need this map. Your destination, like it or not, is death. More cheerfully, life eternal awaits you. Then, you will understand that you only barely understand the vast amount of goodness you have access to in your heart. People will feel happy around you because you are following the map. With regard to competition and racing ... it's just not that kind of map. If you use the map at all, you will advance.

Instructions

We begin by recognizing that studying this map is Alone at the Desk kind of work. This is not a group project. If anyone tries to push themselves in, either in your head or in person, you will simply stop. That is the <u>first instruction</u>. Stop at any intrusion. This map is about you. Only you can figure out how

you should follow it. If you start allowing thoughts of what other people think of you into your head, you have taken the first wrong turn. So, periodically, you will hear a prompt in your head saying, STOP. Then the map will reconfigure and get you back to where you were.

Be strong. Protect yourself out there.

This is really important so we better say more. This instinct for survival has been hard-wired into our brains by the Creator (God). It helps us in different ways in different times. In this time of instant communication, much of which is ugly, we need to jiggle the switch on our self-protection mechanism and get it working to block out all incoming cruelty, human judgment and condemnation. That's our only rule.

Am I saying that there are no other rules or that our breaking of any rules in our yesterdays was a good thing? No. That's not what I'm saying. But life is a roller coaster. We are spiritual beings built for eternity with temporary human bodies. The rules are there for safety. 'Keep your hands in the cart. Keep all valuables in a safe place. Remain under the safety bar.' And who would argue that some of these rules are not reasonable and necessary? But have we ever seen people on television, on a roller coaster?

They all have their hands flying up in the air. "WHEEEEEEE," they seem to be saying. What the heck does that say about the rules?

I guess it says that people, in their excitement and in the exuberance that being on the roller coaster creates, can sometimes break the rules. And by the looks of what we see in

person and on TV, they are, most of them, breaking similar rules. OK. That's our treatment on rules. Over. Done. We can all relax now.

One more instruction. It has been empirically proven that people, without a certain amount of silence, will go insane. As a matter of fact, part of torture sessions conducted by some very sad and disturbed people, (See how I didn't judge them? This is called good modelling), included leaving loud radios playing in terribly grim and dirty rooms so the prisoners would lose their marbles and tell them everything they wanted to know. Not OK. Red card. The point is that we, no less than the prisoners, need silence. Only in silence will we allow our poor little minds to rest. When our minds get the rest we need, we can do the analysis, which, if done correctly, takes us to the first stop on the map, which is coming.

No joke. <u>Second instruction</u>? Find the silence.

Think about it now. Where can you get the silence to follow this map for ten minutes a day, minimum, in your head?

This might be a good time to point out something obvious.

Our soul, that is, the part of us that connects to God and all of our dead relatives, craves stillness and relaxation. We can pray at 100 miles per hour all day long and not feel any better at all. We have to stop and let our minds rest and our poor, tired little bodies breathe.

Try it now. Breathe in deeply. Make sure your stomach goes out and don't worry if you feel it's too big. The effort to hold our stomachs in, all by itself, might just be preventing our bodies from getting something we need. Oxygen. (For the literal readers, exhale now and just keep breathing on your own.)

Let's review.

Reading this map is something you must do alone. If thoughts come into your head about what someone else thinks of you then you say, "STOP." We are not here to talk about rules or who is breaking which ones with whom. We stipulate to the fact that most people seem to be breaking similar rules at least periodically no matter what they are saying. We need to find silence daily or risk going crazy. And our bodies need to concentrate on breathing deeply.

The breathing helps us to slow down and reassures our body that its owner, despite acting like a lunatic sometimes, at least recognizes its basic need for oxygen. If you say you are too busy, then really, you might be a little *too* busy.

Onward.

You are a Good Person, Created to Do Good Things

So the first place on the map, which you may or may not trip over, is as follows: You are a good person created to do good things. This, believe it or not, is really hard for some people to accept. In order to convince them, other people must perform the most extraordinary contortions. Even then some of us have trouble accepting our goodness. And maybe there isn't anyone around telling you that you are a good person created to do good things. But I'm telling you now. And I'm doing this for God.

You are a good person created to do good things.

Now, maybe you are one who says, "Give me a break. I know I'm a good person."

Fine. I believe you. You can skip the next few paragraphs if you really mean it.

Or maybe you are one who says, "Not only am I good, Lady. I'm better than practically everyone I know." (Just to say, don't ignore that little red light flashing that the rest of us can see so clearly).

Or maybe you are one who says, "She does-n't know me very well. I'm actually not such a great person and I've done some terrible things in the past."

Stop! Immediately! Lights are flashing. Sirens are screeching.

"What did I do? What did I do?" you ask in alarm, turning in confused circles.

Spiritual person, this is an emergency. Turn back immediately because there is a caustic and contaminating word in your the text. The word cannot be used right now. We aren't

ready. I haven't laid the ground work. The word is, (full contamination suits and rubber gloves picking up the word) 'past'.

Now run to the window. Go. Go. Go. Throw it out. Picture a hurricane wind taking it to a land of mercy and understanding, far, far, away. Act quickly and with full trust in my instruction.

We are on an educational tour and we are like five-year-olds. We are only at the beginning of our spiritual journey.

Think about it. When five-year-olds visit a fire station, the firemen greet them with smiles and plastic colorful hats. Imagine if they paraded pictures of tragic fires and dead bodies in front of them. The children would cry and be traumatized. Parents would complain. In the same way, when confronted with prior mistakes, we can get really sad and feel helpless, ashamed and really, really angry. (Note the two really's).

You see, we have all been hurt in the past. And some of us have been badly hurt. And this could have caused us to make mistakes that we wish we hadn't made and then we might get angry because to add insult to injury others condemned us for the mistakes without understanding the terrible hurts we experienced so then we might have said, "You know what? I don't care about my mistakes and you stink and I don't like your friends and I HATE that green shirt you are wearing." (Yes. It can get very personal.)

Uh ... see what I mean? Let's stay out of the _____ for now.

Picture dark ugly clouds receding and sunshine and birds coming back.

You are a good person created to do good things.

This sentence, if you believe it, should do two things. And it is a two part sentence so we will break it into two and examine the parts separately. Don't worry. We won't take

too long with it. And this is interesting because it is about you.

Broken up, the first part reads, 'You are a
good person.' Why do I say that? Because I do
not know you so I can rest in the possibility
that there is something good, if deeply hid-
den, about you? No. I say that with confidence
because I know a little about you. How?

I know something about every person on
earth through my study of God.

Amazing. Super magnificent.

God made you. He thought about you and
He created you. He figured, in His knowing,
the world would need someone who looked
like you. He figured that in some way, you
would be necessary in the world right at this
time. You are here because God put you here
and because you are needed here.

If you were not needed here, for some reason, you would be with your dead relatives already. And the dead relatives are important

because just as they affected us during life, perhaps positively, perhaps negatively, most likely in both ways, they affect us now. They want the very best for us.

"They might be in hell," you say.

It's out there, I guess. But I really believe that the barest few actually choose to leave the family of God when they are greeted with the Truth upon death. For purposes of hope and harmony, let's pray they repented of all the bad things they did to you and eventually made it into heaven.

You see, we, to repeat a point, are spiritual beings with temporary human bodies. Our dead relatives are now certain about this. Their doubts are gone, believe me. They are all singing that song by The Monkees, more recently in the movie *Shrek*, called, *"I'm a Believer."* And so, from the next life, they are wishing that you would sink down deeply into your spirituality.

Why do they want this? So that you will stop embarrassing them in front of their new heavenly friends? No. They want this for you so that you can be happy. They, because we all work in the one Spirit if we want goodness for humanity, were hoping I would write this so you could read it. And, despite various obstacles and selfish inclinations, I have complied.

You are a good person.

That Moment in Your Childhood

Go back to a moment when you felt like a good girl or a good boy. You were small, maybe between 3-6 years old. You did something good and someone said, "Good job," and you felt filled with virtue. You had an experience of your goodness. You understood in that moment that truly, you were a contender in this good versus evil battle.

Because I try to be an honest writer, I am going to stop now and try this exercise myself, to make sure it works. But first I want to add a warning. We are not looking for a moment when we felt *better* than anyone else. (Nobody likes those people.) We just felt like a good girl or a good boy and we rejoiced interiorly at this truth.

OK. I tried it. It works. But I think we better go to the age of ten for the memory because if your family of origin was struggling, as some do, you might need the extra four years until someone intervened and thought to tell you that it was not your fault and you were, in fact, a good girl or a good boy.

I have a sad and serious face writing that. People suffer and children can feel confused by the suffering. They are confused because they start off thinking they are lovable and loudly demanding love. (For the record, that's the truth. We are all extremely lovable.) When children get hurt, over time, they get perplexed. 'Why don't they love me?' they wonder.

But children are good at loving so no matter who hurts them, they forgive. And when it is their family, parents or siblings or what have you, who hurt them, they feel compassion and sorrow. They want to forgive and they do forgive but someone needs to ask for their forgiveness. This makes their confusion go away. It's pretty basic.

If someone says, "I'm sorry I hurt you," or even, "I'm sorry you were hurt by this situation," the child can make sense out of that. Mistakes are not confusing. Children make them all the time when they color outside of the lines. As children, we understand mistakes. And it's not until later that we get really mad about it all and start acting out and taking revenge. Understandable. Truly. And if I understand all of this, a writer of average intelligence, can you imagine how much God understands? God is way too smart to make casual judgments against people for external mistakes they make from a place of internal pain.

You are a good person. The dead relatives are trying to get me to focus.

Back to the moment in your childhood when you felt like a good person ... FREEZE! You are that same person. Right now, today, you are that very same, exact, DNA-match, person. And all of that goodness is within you, all of that potential, all of that craving for virtue. And when you die, you will feel exactly like a child again. Because just like we were born into time at conception, we will experience a different process and depart from time, entering timelessness.

This is a good thing. Trust me. Life is really

hard away from heaven. Picture coming into time at conception to be like temporarily wearing heavy ski boots. (Sorry, skiers. I hated skiing. I realize some of you feel free careening down mountains on things with no brakes but it didn't do it for me.) Both conception and birth are joyous events, I know, because people are entering time for a purpose and a plan. And possibly their parents want the baby.

You are a good person.

Maybe this is a hard sell for you or maybe you always knew it. Regardless, we have to move on.

I know I said the sentence was breaking up into two and it is, really, but I need to emphasize one middle word. The word is created. I have to give it a quick treatment. Yes, you were created. You were contemplated and Voila! God made you. He adores you. You are like His best mud pie. Remember mud pies? We made them because our mothers wouldn't let us mess up the kitchen and, as little chefs, we had to bake. So we did it outside with mom's best pie pans. And our best mud pie ... well, some of us still remember what it looked like.

That's how God views you, as one of His finest moments as Creator.

You are a good person, created (by God).

So what happens now? Should you nomadically wander the world wearing sandals and robes? Preaching at people? Hatin' on the bad ones'? Torturing everyone with the concept of sin? Ranting about hell? Scrutinizing people in the hopes that you'll find their worst mistakes? OF THEIR _____ ????

(That was an intentional distortion of what a holy person does.)

I don't think so. It's not that simple and it's not that easy. God has a far greater challenge in mind for you. Because you were created to do good, and because you are still temporarily in time, you have to stop right now. Long pause. (I'm picturing you frozen like in the statues game. See? You are still in time.) We have to stop torturing ourselves about the _____ and terrifying ourselves about the future. Here's why. **We were created to do good.**

This is very serious. And it's the second part of the sentence. God created us to do good. Yesterday? Well, I don't think so because yesterday is over. Tomorrow? Well, God is not irrational. He is smarter than all of us so I hardly believe he would ask the impossible which is that we would do good in the future when we are stuck in the present. That makes no sense at all. We have to do good today *for* the future. And it's time to stop saying that someday we are going to turn over a new leaf and become good people. Do it now. Fast.

"AHHHHHHH."

I hear the primal screams. "We knew it. We knew it would come to this. It was a trick document, acting all nice and friendly. But really, she wants us to give up our coffee, cigarettes, alcohol, sex, shopping, money, gambling, grudges, boat, etc."

Reader, be fair. I didn't say anything about giving anything up. That is like Lent. I said, "Turn over a new leaf and be a good person." We are not going to start giving things up right now. Maybe later, you will have to stop smoking if your family asks you. I don't know. It is none of my business. What I am saying is that right now, you have to think of one nice thing you can do for someone else that you wouldn't ordinarily do. If it has to do with forgiving someone for something really mean they did, well let's just say the dead relatives would be proud. But by doing one more thing than you would ordinarily do in the course of your day, an act of kindness, mercy or for-giveness, then you are turning over a new leaf. You are stretching spiritually and that's what you are supposed to be doing in time.

"I'm nice already, Lady," you might be saying.

That's true. You are a good person. We've stipulated to that. But you have been hurt, remember? And so, humanity being what it is, maybe you need to forgive someone for something. If we do it together, it won't be as hard.

Think of someone who has hurt you. Now think of something sad that might have happened to that person, as a child. Picture that person's sadness and confusion at being hurt.

(We picture the hurter as a child because it's often the only way we can forgive and let's face it, we are all children in God's eyes.)

And now picture meeting the person in heaven. They are so sorry. Their face is sad because they understand how badly you were hurt. They say, "I'm so sorry."

And what will you say? "Get out of heaven?"

I don't think so. You'll be really embarrassed if you say that. We'll all be embarrassed.

Most likely you will say, "It's OK. It was very confusing down there in time. I forgive you and I was just kidding about your green shirt."

OK, good person. You can see that the point of this writing is being met. It's reflecting you, not me. The map is intended to take you to a place where you are safe and there is truth. We aren't there yet but we are making progress. You cannot hold grudges and be happy. So turning over a new leaf includes thinking of anyone who hurt you and admitting that maybe someone hurt them first and, like an urban myth, they passed it on.

To review?

You are a good person.

(I'm so sorry. But it's huge. I have to keep repeating it, especially if you are addicted, in prison or you are getting separated or divorced or you've just been indicted, arrested, fired, failed another test, detained in immigration or crashed into the guy in front of you because he stopped and you were on your **_cell phone_** or a bank foreclosed on your house, or someone just yelled at you a lot, or you just made a sexual mistake. (The little print is me respecting your privacy).

You are a good person, (created by God).

You were created to do good, not yesterday, not tomorrow, but right now, quickly, before you die. It doesn't matter that you may always have been a good person. Or that you think you are great. Or that you think you are horrible. You are a good person, created to do good, and God expects you to try now. A good place to start is by thinking of someone who hurt you and trying to forgive them.

To end this part, I want to make an observation. Prepare to be stunned.

You are probably not the best person in the world. You are probably not the worst. You, like me, are probably somewhere in the middle. And that is the next stop on the map. It's the place where you say, "I am just me, somewhere in the middle."

I Am Just Me, Somewhere In the Middle

Why is this a good place? Because it might just be the place where you stop trying to rate yourself, evaluate yourself, judge yourself, justify yourself, condemn yourself or feel like you are a failure. You are not God. You are just a person, doing his or her best

to get through life without hurting yourself or too many other people. If you failed in the _____, it's OK because that's finished. You are still in time which means you are in the present. Which means you can still do good things. If you are already doing a ton of good, try to squeeze one more little thing out of yourself. Because this writing is a map, we all have to move and keep moving. If we don't, I will feel like a failure as a mapologist. (I know. I can't remember it and I actually like my word better.) So get out there, or in there, (head), and do something good today, something that would make that child who felt like a good girl or boy proud.

One more thing for today. Say to yourself, repeatedly, out loud, but not in public, "I for-give you today, _add your name_, for not being perfect." And every morning you could say to yourself, with great kindness, "Good morning, _add your name_. Welcome to another imper-fect day starring you."

Let's see ... in the interest of flow, you are a good person, created, (by God), to do good AND you are imperfect.

Can we reconcile that? Our imperfection and also our mandate to act favorably upon the human family?

I think we have to. I mean ... if we are going to make any progress at all, we will have to accept our imperfection. Sometimes, we take a bath in our imperfection. We are confounded by it. Confused. We simply stop altogether. We either call this a nervous breakdown or a spiritual awakening depending on who we hang around with but there comes a time when we crash into the reality that we are not perfect today, that we made some truly spectacular mistakes in the _____, and, at best, we will only be able to contribute an offering that is ... take a wild guess ... imperfect, in the future.

Big sigh.

Of relief if you are wound too tightly or dismay if you are too relaxed or frozen. Dismay because I am saying that you might be using your awareness of imperfection as an excuse not to contribute. Excuse might be an important word for you. Have a look at it and check. Maybe not, but if it is ... Up on your feet, spiritual being. Everybody has to move.

Regarding a possible crisis at the realization that you are imperfect? See it coming, beloved brother or sister. Expect it. And when it happens, look back on the map and remember what I said about keeping other people out of your journey, especially condemning know-it-alls. (Bad modelling by imperfect spiritual person.)

Important safety tip. Don't judge the judgers or you become a judger. They do serve a purpose. Think of the crashed car that state troopers put on the side of the highway by the speed sign. They hope this shows us how *not* to do it. If you cannot be the good example, you may end up being the horrible warning. And being honest? We are all that guy/girl on some days. To repeat, don't judge the judgers or you become one of them and don't blame them for your lack of spiritual progress. Keep moving despite them.

WARNING:

DON'T JUDGE THE JUDGERS

**The judgers could actually use the next chapter.

I Am Imperfect

Imperfect.

We give it its own stop on the map. This is the stop that confirms that an imperfect spiritual being is resting here.

Am I trying to be mean? Upsetting? Am I trying to drive you away? Or, am I cleverly offering you freedom? Am I trying to say,

"FREEDOM ANYONE?"

"Spiritual being, rest peacefully and properly into your humanity. Perhaps for the first time." Breathe deeply, (watching that the stomach moves) repeatedly, calmly.

It is true. Your imperfection has been factored in. The universe has built-in allowances, which, like shock absorbers, absorb your false starts, your stumbles, fumbles and ridiculous tackles. Many a football game was won which included incomplete passes and penalties. In one sport, I think basketball, an action against a person is called a personal foul or maybe it's a technical foul. I like that.

That's the more serious kind, as it should be.

It's like saying, "Here look, Tommy, we are willing to put up with a lot in the name of the sport but now you are crossing lines." Picture a stern face on the referee. Deep frown. You remember. Holding up the red card? Putting you in the penalty box? Rotating you out? I'm seriously cross-pollinating my sports but I'm trying to please everyone. And I think you get it. After all, it's about you. And it's OK that you failed yesterday (note successful avoidance of the truly bad four letter word _____). Today? You are succeeding. Why? Because you are still with me on the journey.

Now if this piece is required reading for a course, you might not be succeeding. I can't tell. And it's none of my business. But if you are engaging your intellect by actually looking at yourself with even the smallest degree of curiosity, then you are succeeding even though someone compelled you to read this.

Only you can know. Uh ... you and the dead relatives. They are pretty plugged in, not to intimidate you.

The reason we need you, universally speaking, to take this journey is that together, a bunch of imperfect people can do unbelievably good things. The key is *unity.*

Think of World War II. My dad was an American Marine. My siblings and I thought (through forced listening) one heck of a lot about WWII. In that war, a bunch of truly imperfect people banded together and pushed back at a really sad/unstable guy and the astonishingly brazen campaign he began.

Now here listen, if you were on the losing side of that war, and I know some of you were, don't feel badly. It was in the _____, and we, the Allies, did some astonishingly stupid things too that we are not proud of. People get nutty, alone and in groups and that's just the truth. But we, the Allies, imperfect though we were, succeeded that time. Because ... we were all the same? No. We were quite different. We were different people of different genders, different nationalities, different colors and different religions. We had in common a cause which we believed was so important that it overrode all of our separateness. We, from what I heard, (repeatedly), put all division into the pot of

the collective goal and made the stew that won the war.

My friends, (if you are still reading, I am thinking of you as extremely tolerant friends), what we do counts. We have to put our name on the board of humanity, so to speak. I am protecting your right to be heard by writing this. Optimistic? I don't think so. Because, remember, I know something about you, not through some creepy technology, but through my study of God. I know that you were created (by God) to do good in some way. I know that the world needs goodness, really bad. (Te he.) And if you are feeling powerless because of your imperfection, or you have unplugged from the spiritual part of you, we, like Houston (*Apollo 13* reference), have a problem.

Plug in, spiritual being.

Let's allow, just for a moment, (read slowly, in a musing tone) that there is an infinite purpose, ordered to the good, which ordained your existence.

People might get annoyed here. Why? Various reasons. Some think that no good God could allow anything bad and they get really mad because of things like earthquakes and tsunamis and Auschwitz. They say, "How could a good God allow those bad things?"

I get the point. Suffering is sad. The confusion comes though, from a misunderstanding of God, free will and time. (Darn that timelessness concept.) Man is given the freedom to choose goodness or badness. Period. He gets to pick. Sometimes, maybe through woundedness, he chooses poorly and other people get hurt. An extreme example of this is something like Auschwitz. Allowing people to do good or bad things is fair and consistent with the gift of free will and the freedom to make choices. This is why we do our hard work, so that we make good choices which do not hurt ourselves or others.

As for the natural catastrophes, time is limited. And the earth is moving through time. I mean, if we stayed in the prehistoric times, yes, we would still have dinosaurs but we wouldn't have you.

And this is about you.

Remember, suffering is one part of time, for you, for me, and for the dinosaurs now deceased like the dead relatives.

Wonder with me, if there is an infinite purpose buried in your today. If there is, and I'm just asking the question, what might it be? (The parents here are saying, "Yeah, my infinite purpose is to cook dinner." Moms and Dads, you are right. Parents are the best!)

We acknowledged our imperfection and agreed that despite our imperfections we recognized some goodness, as evidenced by that moment in our childhoods when someone had the courtesy to tell us we were good. We agreed that we were humanly present in time as spiritual beings (Maybe that was me. That's aggressive of me, insisting that we are all spiritual beings but I really believe it. I do.) So what is the point if not to do something today that is good externally, in addition to the good that we already did earlier?

A question.

Are we, humanity, in a spiritual war, a huge battle of good versus evil? Is that what I'm saying? Yes. But wait. I don't believe we are involved in anything unusual. Look back. Human beings are always fighting. Human conflict seems to occur regularly, like the earthquakes and tsunamis. The bad example seems to be a periodic negative offering from one generation to the next. I think that thinking of the war of good versus evil can be OK, but I think that some people hide behind the concept, identifying it accurately in others but ignoring it in themselves.

Breathe in and out. Slowly. Steadily.

I think we were created (by God) to advance spiritually. And I don't think a spiritually advanced person is out there committing a ton of personal fouls. I give anyone doing that a red card. So … making a decision to bomb Pearl Harbor? Bang out of order. Dropping nuclear bombs on civilians in Hiroshima? Bang, bang out of order.

Easy for me to say. I'm not there. Both the Japanese and Americans had their opinions.

And now we love each other. See? Human conflict, generally speaking, is temporary. And to focus, those weren't my calls. I cannot judge the people. But I am here, in today, and there are choices which are mine and who knows how many will be affected by my decisions?

Spiritual beings, what we do counts!!

Get to the place on the map that says I Am Important.

I Am Important

Now. Look around your day from that place. What should you do next?

For example, I ask you. Who encouraged little Helen Keller? Annie Sullivan. Did Annie Sullivan feel like a person who would enable another person to pioneer communication for disabled people? Did she feel super impor-

tant? I bet she didn't. I bet she felt like any other teacher. And I bet she took one look at Helen Keller before she connected with her and I bet she thought two things. 1) This job is way out of my league, and 2) I stink as a teacher. But Annie Sullivan had a purpose, a hope in her existence, and she got on with it.

Both Annie Sullivan and Helen Keller are big shots to me.

Who cooked dinner for Saint Damien? I'm thinking his mother. Did she feel like a big shot? I wouldn't think so, given their ordinary social status, but she did provide, along with his Dad (fyi Dad's are huge, even when they cannot be with their children) and siblings, care and feeding, never mind formation, for the one guy who decided to share exile with lepers. (In fairness, other priests volunteered, too, but Damien's offer was accepted by his Superior, the Bishop said 'Go', and he not only went, he stayed, as did, later, a group of religious sisters from America).

Damien's mother, like Damien, is a big shot to me.

Now, spiritual beings, who is counting on you? Who is hoping you will think about them? Who could use a little bit of you? Take some time each day to consider this. You have a minimum of ten minutes a day in silence, we agreed. (Technically, you might not have agreed with me, but you would if you knew how important it was. We are starting at ten but I hope you'll gradually increase the time. Silence is everything in the spiritual life and we feed our body, which is temporary. We should feed our souls, too.)

Anyway, in the silence you are saying, 'I, though imperfect, am important. What do I need to do next?'

I think we need an unscheduled stop. I'm just thinking of you, taking your ten minutes in silence, and I'm worried, like a mother who watches children heading for school with a storm cloud coming.

'They'll get wet', she's thinking.

The Bird Sanctuary

I draw your attention to the left. This is just for learning but it is experiential learning so we will like it. There is a building. It says Bird Sanctuary on the sign. We walk in. We're walking, looking, like a third grade class. We see all kinds of birds. They are gorgeous, really, flying around, singing. There are trees, pretty lights and POW. One of the birds drops down onto the floor, stunned. We look around, mouths open, and there stands **'one of us'**. On any day **'one of us'** could be 'any of us' obviously.

'One of us' is holding a sling shot. He shot the bird. We say, all together, kindly, **'"One of us'**, please put that sling shot away. These birds aren't targets. This is their home, their safe place. No shooting at the birds."

Some people, right?

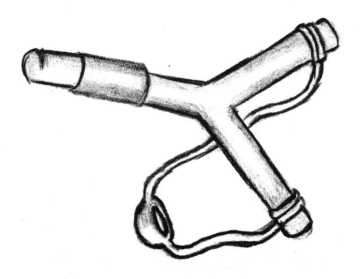

Now, in our Catholic Church we have a teaching about something called our conscience. You are thinking, 'Here she goes. It was a matter of time'. But this is huge for you. You see, our Catechism, (Possible unfamiliar word. Don't worry. It's the collection of our spiritual teachings in a book.), says that *"conscience is man's secret core and his sanctuary. There he is alone with God whose voice echoes in his depths"* (1776 CCC).

I'm telling you the truth. People are confused about this. Your conscience is like a place you go where you can rest in the truth and be safe. It's your sanctuary. There is nobody else in your conscience but God, who loves you totally and understands you perfectly. And if you are there, resting, and **'One of us'** makes an entrance with a slingshot, you say, "Get out. No unwelcome visitors."

It's quiet and calm in your conscience. It might just be the only safe place on earth for us spiritual beings. And spending time in silence in our conscience with God might be the one thing that keeps us sane because I promise you this, only in your conscience will you be truly understood. No person on earth will ever totally get you. Only God totally gets you. Trust me. We all feel this way. A little alone and a little afraid. The sooner we accept this, the sooner we can stop expecting other people to fix this for us.

Take the Silence. Get the peace.

10 MINUTES OF SILENCE

Now, mostly what we do in our conscience is rest and recover. Picture yourself as a hypothermia victim with warm blankets all around you. A rescue worker is adjusting the dial on the warm blankets to recover you a little at a time, safely. You are not thinking right now of any failures in the _____. You are being gentle with yourself and thinking of all that you do right, every day.

I'm not joking. This may go against everything you know about your conscience but your conscience is your sanctuary. I am, awkwardly at times, giving it to you straight. If you want to take care of yourself spiritually, then you should **spend time each day thinking about what it is you are doing right. Then do more of it**.

It might be helpful for us to picture our conscience as a room filled with pictures of all the good things we have done in our lives hanging all over the walls.

With regard to mistakes and sins? How does a good person, created to do good, deal with their mistakes and sins? Excellent ques-

tion, spiritual being. I have a suggestion. (You figured I would.)

Try this formula.

'I was **afraid,** and then I did this, (<u>add your own fouls/mistakes/sling shot efforts</u>).

'I was **badly hurt,** and then I did this, (<u>again, add your mistake</u>).

Or 'I was **addicted, confused, terrified, devastated, upside down, unbearably angry, etc.** and then I did this and that and the other, (<u>spectacular wrong action or pattern of wrong actions in painful period of your life, which, if not over, is now passing by the second</u>).

Am I saying these things to make you feel guilty? No. I'm not like that. I'm saying these things to free you so that you can sit quietly with God (who created you) and be super happy about all that you are doing right each day, in your family, in your work, in your prison cell (whatever that is for you) and in the world. Spiritual being, if you are like me, and I think you are, then you are probably getting it mostly right, instead of mostly wrong. At the very least, there is certainly something you are doing that's good, right and commendable.

Make the mistakes smaller in your head and enjoy the pictures on the wall of your conscience of each loving act, each decision for honesty and each moment where you respected another person, especially if it was in a parking lot of a shopping center at Christmas! Or a rehab. Or a prison. Then you will WANT to go to your conscience. It will be like a sun holiday, or a park for you.

OK. Of everything, I really hope you get the concept of being safe and loved in your conscience. It will change your life.

We're moving.

The next stop on the map, moving from the destination of I am Important and the Bird Sanctuary is North, straight up on every map. Start walking and I'll tell you where we are going later.

Sometimes life is painful and we are tempted against it. By that I mean that good days come and go and sometimes bad days come and stay. Doesn't it seem that way? That we get stuck in quick-sand-like places and we can't get out? And when this happens, we are like Dorothy in The Wizard of Oz. She drags that dog all over the yellow brick road, picking up some nice, if odd, friends, and pining for somewhere else. Dorothy wants to go home. We all do. But home is a mirage, I'm afraid, at least while we are stuck in time.

I'm saying that I think that we put a lot of stock in being somewhere else. We say, "If only I were somewhere else I would be happy. If only I were with someone else I would be happy. If only I had this other pair of shoes I would be happy. Or, if only I could pay my bills I would be happy." *

But friends, think about it. There were times when we were somewhere else, with someone else, wearing different shoes and paying our bills and we were still unhappy.

"Yeah? Well it was better than this," you might be saying.

To which I would respond, "Possibly, but possibly you have also been in worse situations than today and possibly, tomorrow could take a serious downturn and you will be in a worse situation than now."

I'm not trying to depress you. I'm just making pragmatic small talk until we get to the next place. OK. Thank God. Here it is.

It's called Life is About Now.

Optional Exercise in Perspective

*When the embarrassing but inevitable fog of self-pity rolls in, try this formula, kind of as a joke but also as an exercise: If only I wasn't buried under ten tons of rubble after that darn earthquake I would be happy.

Life is About Now

We are at the next place on the map. We need to really sit and contemplate this place. Let's call it NOW for short. Let's take another deep breath and put the two last places together. *I Am Important* and *Life is About Now*. What we do in NOW affects a couple things. One, it affects us. Two, it af-

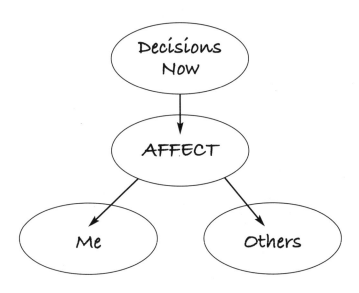

fects everyone around us.

How?

Well, given the universal truth of cause and effect and the reality of quantum physics, a good decision in NOW will have a ripple effect, an impact. We are all acting on the universe in some way, good or bad.

Neither is not an answer. You can't sit on the fence of life. If you do, it's called ambivalence and that, my friends, should be the worst four letter word out there, even worse than the _____.

The first person affected by your decision in the place of NOW is you. And this is about you. Please read this carefully. Do you want to be happy? Or do you want to be sad? Picture the two words up on the wall written on big buttons that you can push. SAD is a red button. Green is the HAPPY button. Close your eyes. Reach up and push one.

This is serious. You are deciding. Push one. OK. It lit up.

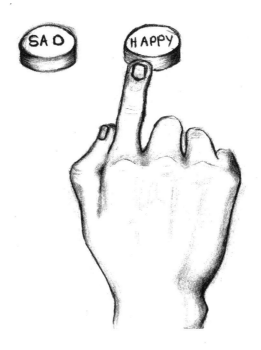

If you pushed SAD then you have to live sad. (Yes, I have my hands on my hips.) Don't be false about it. Don't act like everything is OK. You pushed SAD and now you have to live it.

Picture the referee who gave you the red card. You are trying not to laugh at him because your friend is standing behind him making fun of him. You, trying to be serious, accidently smile a little. The ref says, "Wipe that smile off your face, Mr."

I am like that ref, only nice, saying, "If you pushed the red button, don't smile" (good friend). If you pick SAD and you want SAD, then you have to live SAD-ly. You have chosen.

Now, maybe you are thinking, "Lady, I just picked a button randomly and I hate the color green so I picked red. Plus, I hate my life so I might as well pick SAD. I don't necessarily want to live sad forever, though."

Well, I would say to you then that you

should think carefully when you press the buttons in NOW. Because just like what you do counts in life, the button you push every morning counts in NOW. And like the movie about a baseball field in the middle of nowhere when a voice says, quite eerily, "If you build it, they will come," I am saying to you, "If you push it, it will happen."

Push the green button, HAPPY, and smile an obligatory smile for heaven's sake. Life is hard enough when you are in time.

Stay with me. We're moving again. We just pushed the green button that says, HAPPY, and now we have to live it, smiling and feeling ridiculous. Fake it until you make it, as a teenager recently told me about making homemade secret-recipe Chinese chicken. (I, myself, felt it was a possible copyright violation to have the recipe up on the internet but I suppose it's like carrying a knock-off purse.)

So we, in our recent history, have been to the place of I Am Important, we have travelled through the place of Life is About Now and we have chosen there, HAPPY and we are walking again, wearing a smile, possibly phony like the knock-off purse, but we are faking it until we make it.

If you are now thinking I am reaching over your shoulder and pushing buttons against your will like the annoying friend helping you with your computer, I am sorry. But really, if you picked SAD deliberately then I think I have to park you on the side lines. I'm benching you, but only for a minute because to be honest, for some people, the HAPPY button doesn't seem to work even though they keep picking it. And that stinks. My face is sad and serious. We have to get your HAPPY button working. But even if it doesn't work now, keep pushing it and decide you WILL be happy, if it kills you. Trust me. You'll get used to it if you keep doing it. And I'm not really benching you. I was just kidding you. (Bad modelling by imperfect, smiling, spiritual being.)

Let's move.

The Train (Mandatory)

We're walking, walking, and we are arriving at a train station. It's crowded, but orderly, like in Switzerland.

NOT like in this other place that I won't name that scared me almost to death. They've never heard of lines there and God help them they just PRESS forward until various random people get popped through the doors of trains and I guess those are the ones going. You have to hang on to your purses and clutch your travel companions and just let the experience happen because you need the train, you know?

So here there is order and there are trains. And you are getting on one. Your time for choice is over. You are travelling on this day. Did I mention that this day was way up in the right hand corner of the map? This is your death day. When I say death, I smile serenely. It seems perverse of me, I know. But I am using my spiritual eyes when I study this place on the map and all I see is that the trains are clean and bright, the people boarding don't have to make choices anymore and there is relief in that. They are simply getting on the trains and sitting down in the clean, comfortable seats.

There can be a little trouble at this station. Here's why.

Sometimes people make decisions for other people that it's time to get on the train. We are not supposed to do that, in any way, shape or form. You can disagree. I don't care. This is a Ten Commandment issue and this is not about me. It's about all of us. And the train that is death is one that has names on the seats. It's arranged by Someone Else before the people get on, like the more expensive airlines and the classrooms with totally organized teachers.

Now … what happens when someone drags someone to the train and throws them on? Well, the holy people working on the train, who are like the old W__ mart greeters, looking very seriously at the one throwing the person on the train, make room, of course. What can they do? They receive the dead person with love and smiles and place him comfortably in his chair with some extra stuff to compensate for the trauma of getting thrown on.

But, being honest? We cannot pretend this is Plan A.

(And no jumping on to the train either. Let the painful moments pass. They will. I promise.)

The good news is, as an imperfect spiritual being, you, like the child coloring outside of the lines, can say, "I'm sorry," if you threw someone on the train. And the rest of us will forgive you because we have our own mistakes, too, so we know all about mistakes and why they are made.

For example, sometimes people reach over other people's shoulders and pick their SAD button through their actions and then the others live out sad lives that they wouldn't have picked. But I'm telling you in this writing that you do get to pick. And frankly, you have to pick. Not choosing for yourself is wrong. So remember, those people pushing your buttons aren't the boss of you. Maybe you could pick HAPPY now and then go more cheerfully from the place that is NOW, for short, to the train station that is death.

It's up to you, though. It's definitely your pick.

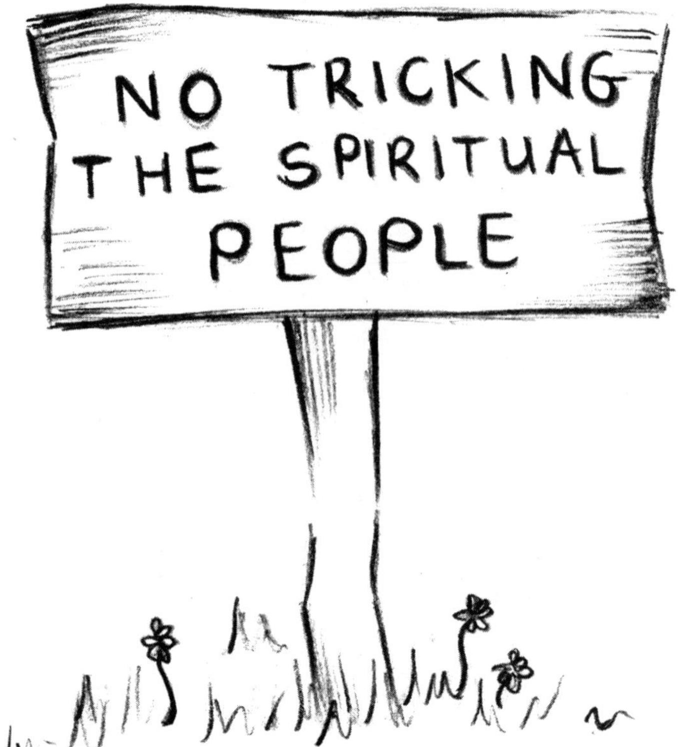
NO TRICKING
THE SPIRITUAL
PEOPLE

Summary

Don't be tricked. You are a spiritual being, living humanity for a limited time. You are probably getting more right than wrong. You have choices, no matter what circumstances you are living. You can choose to live from your humanity and ignore the spiritual part of you. Or you can say to your spiritual side,

"I get you, spiritual side. You should be doing the driving." Say to yourself, "If I look at life spiritually, it will all eventually slide into focus. My decisions won't be as complicated and the outcome will be, mysteriously, part of a good plan for every person ever created (by God)."

Big sigh of relief. I'm wrapping this up.

So now I thank you for taking this trek with me, spiritual being. I recognize you in the universe. I love you and I am proud of all that you have survived in this weird and wonderful world. If I travel before you, then I will be waiting for you on the train when you get there. And if you get there before me, well, maybe sit next to me, please, so I feel like I have a friend, and we can talk together about how hard it was during our time in time.

The end.

Possible Next Stop

Eucharistic Adoration Chapel

If this writing made you frustrated because it was random or confusing at times, maybe just overlook that. Because the writing could only be imperfect given that I wrote it. You see, the writing is just like you and me. The writing was never supposed to be perfect. It was only supposed to make a contribution. And this writing is not about me being a good writer. It's about you being a bona fide, card carrying, mystical and spiritual person living in time, with the rest of us, for a short time.

And if you are Catholic or not, practicing or not, Christian, agnostic, atheist or what have you, we offer you a safe, uncomplicated place to go. Find the nearest Eucharistic Adoration Chapel and rest there. There will be nobody challenging you, asking your status or demanding your papers. Nobody will care about your _____. It will be you and God.

(We believe God is there.)

There you can breathe deeply (making sure your stomach moves) and rest in your spiritual self. Everyone is welcome to come and visit with God. We promise you silence and peace.

Now I'm really done. See you on the train.

Author's Note

This writing comes with an earnest desire to offer spiritual encouragement to people of all faiths and none.

This writing represents only my personal thoughts.

This writing is my contribution in the period of time designated as the Year of Faith.

For more spiritual reading, please go to www.gabrielpressusa.com or read *Climbing the Mountain* published by Direction for Our Times and available at www.directionforourtimes.org.